THE POWER OF ENTHUSIASM

Featuring the story of Theodore Roosevelt

Authors
Phyllis Colonna
Della Mae Rasmussen

Art Illustrator
Stephen P. Krause

Editor, Layout and Research
Beatrice W. Friel

THE POWER OF
ENTHUSIASM

Featuring the story of Theodore Roosevelt

Advisors
Paul and Millie Cheesman
Mark Ray Davis
Rodney L. Mann, Jr.
Roxanne Shallenberger
Dale T. Tingey

Publisher
Steven R. Shallenberger

Director and Correlator
Lael J. Woodbury

AN EAGLE SYSTEMS
INTERNATIONAL
PUBLICATION
ANTIOCH, CALIFORNIA

The Power of Enthusiasm
Copyright © 1981 by
Power Tales
Eagle Systems International
P.O. Box 1229
Antioch, California 94509

ISBN: 0-911712-90-3

Library of Congress Catalog No.: 81-50864

First Edition

Lithographed in USA by
COMMUNITY PRESS, INC.

A member of
The American Bookseller's Association
New York, New York

Dedicated to enthusiastic children everywhere.

THEODORE ROOSEVELT

Theodore Roosevelt was born 27 October 1858 in New York City to Theodore and Martha Bullock Roosevelt. Teddy, as he was called, was the second of four children in a wealthy, aristocratic family. As a child he was sickly and suffered greatly from asthma. He was also extremely near-sighted.

Being determined to overcome his weakness, Teddy spent many hours working out in a gymnasium his father equipped for him. He also took long walks in the fresh air to improve his health. These walks nurtured what was to become a lifelong interest in nature.

By sheer force of will Teddy did other things to overcome his physical handicaps: he became a good rider, a good boxer, and a good marksman. Because of his perseverance in strenuous exercise and outdoor living, he was able to overcome his physical deficiencies. As he grew older, he developed a magnificent physique.

But body strength wasn't his only interest. He also had a keen mind and, while still young, developed a passion for reading. Later, when he attended school at Harvard, he was elected to Phi Beta Kappa, America's leading scholarship fraternity. Before graduating in 1880, he started writing a *History of the Naval War of 1812* because he considered the current publications on this subject unreliable and prejudiced. Love of truth and fair play was such a strong part of his character that he felt compelled to write an accurate account of that important event. The work was well-written and completed shortly after his graduation.

From there he went on to study at Columbia Law School. In 1881, at the age of twenty-three, Teddy was elected to the New York legislature. In this position he became well-known as an enemy of corruption and a leader for reform.

Teddy married Alice Hathaway Lee of Boston. In February of 1884 Alice gave birth to a baby daughter. Twelve hours later Alice died, and within hours of he￢ death Teddy's mother died of typhoid fever.

Following this double tragedy, Teddy completed his political obligations and retired to his ranches in Dakota Territory. He spent the next two years ranching, hunting, and writing his experiences.

In 1886 he returned to New York City and politics. After an unsuccessful campaign for mayor Teddy went to Europe. While in London he married Edith Kermit Carow, a woman he had known since childhood. They had four sons and a daughter.

When Teddy was thirty-one, President Harrison appointed him a member of the Civil Service Commission. While in this position he became very unpopular with crooked politicians, and he made the Civil Service Law a force for good government. He then resigned this position to become Police Commissioner for New York. After a long, hard struggle he cleaned up the police force and was then invited to become Assistant Secretary of the Navy.

When the Spanish-American War broke out, Teddy resigned his position as Assistant Secretary of the Navy and became lieutenant-colonel in a volunteer cavalry unit, later nicknamed the Rough Riders. He served with distinction in this unit, and at the end of the war he returned to politics.

In 1898 Teddy was elected governor of New York state. As governor he investigated and dealt with racketeering, dishonest enterprises, and doubtful business ethics.

In 1900 he was elected Vice President of the United States. In September of the following year President McKinley was murdered and Teddy became President. Among his accomplishments as President, he took a firm stand against trusts, he forced settlement of a coal strike that had threatened to paralyze industry, and he played an active part in pushing the construction of the Panama Canal.

After finishing out President McKinley's term of office, Teddy was elected in 1904 by a vast majority for a four year term. It was during this term that he received the Nobel Peace Prize for his services in bringing about peace between Russia and Japan.

Despite nationwide desire to draft him for a third term, Teddy declined the nomination and retired from the office of President in 1909.

After his retirement he spent a year in Africa hunting big game, after which he went on an exploring expedition to South America.

Teddy, a prominent statesman, naturalist, author, explorer, and soldier, remained actively involved in political issues until his death on 6 January 1919.

Have you ever noticed how many great and famous people were born poor? Sometimes it almost seems a person *has* to be born poor if he wants to become great and famous! But that isn't really true. I'm going to tell you about a man who was born rich, but he grew up to be one of America's favorite presidents. His name was Theodore Roosevelt.

What's that you say? You want to know who *I* am? My name is Bucky Beaver, and Teddy Roosevelt has always been a special friend of mine. In fact, he was a friend of all the creatures of the fields and woods. He had many qualities of a great hero—courage, honesty, caring—but if I had to choose one I liked above all the rest, I would choose his enthusiasm. Whatever Teddy did, he did with all his heart. That is what enthusiasm means, you know. Enthusiasm is really believing in what you do, and doing it with all your heart.

Teddy was born October 27, 1858, in his family's big mansion in New York. Now you might think because he was born rich he didn't have any problems, but that wasn't the case at all. It's true that he had a beautiful home with many servants and a family that loved him—but he had one big problem that no one else could take care of for him. In spite of everything the doctors could do, he was always weak and sick. In fact, he was even too sick to go to school, so his father had special teachers come to his home to help him study.

"Dad, I don't want to spend my whole life being sick," Teddy said to his father one day. "I want to swim and ride horses and do everything the other boys do."

"Of course you do, Ted," his father told him. "That's what I want for you, too. I would make you strong if I could, but I can't."

"Well, isn't there something I can do to make myself strong?" Teddy asked. "What do people do to make themselves strong and healthy?"

His father looked at him thoughtfully. "Fresh air and lots of good exercise are important when people want to be strong," he said. "Eating the right food is important, too, and getting enough sleep."

So Teddy and his father began making a plan for Teddy to follow. Mr. Roosevelt built a gym on the back porch of their large home, and every morning Ted would get up early and work hard to build up his strength. At first he could hardly do anything at all!

In one end of the gym was a tall pole that reached from the floor to the very high ceiling. When Teddy first started his plan, no matter how hard he tried he couldn't climb even a few feet off the floor.

But every morning he worked and worked. He worked with such enthusiasm that the day finally came when he climbed all the way to the top. He let out such a yell that his mother came running from the other end of the house.

"Look, Mom!" he called excitedly. "I can touch the ceiling with one hand!" His mother was very happy to see him getting so strong, but she sometimes thought he took too many chances!

"Oh Theodore," she sighed. "Will you please come down from there? If the Lord didn't take good care of you, you'd have been killed long ago!"

14

Every summer the Roosevelt family left their home in the city and went to stay in their home in the country. This fit right in with Teddy's plans because he was determined to get as much fresh air and outdoor exercise as he possibly could.

Almost every morning he was outside as soon as the sun was up. Sometimes—especially at first—it was hard for him to walk and play. In fact, sometimes it was even hard for him to get his breath. He had a disease called asthma, and asthma makes it difficult to breathe.

But remember that everything Teddy did, he did with all his heart. He had so much enthusiasm for his get-well plan that no matter how hard it was to keep trying, he just wouldn't give up. Every day he found he could walk a little farther than the day before. Soon instead of only walking, sometimes he was running—and each day he seemed a little stronger.

"Today I hiked a mile across the fields!" he told his father one evening. "By next week I will be walking two miles!"

Teddy came to love the outdoors. By summer's end he could hike many miles every day. He came to know the fields and woods as well as he knew his own gym back in the city. He learned the names of all the plants and animals, and he spent hours studying the birds. He could whistle their

songs, and he knew where they built their nests. He learned to sit so
quietly while he studied them that they came very close to him.

Teddy's father was proud of all the hard things his son had learned to do.
The two of them spent many hours together, and little by little his father
taught Teddy to swim, ride horses, and row a boat on the lake.

Now mind you, this didn't all happen in a day or a month. In fact, it didn't even happen in one year. But every summer and every winter Teddy followed his plan with all his heart. In the city he worked in his gym, and in the country he rode horses, hiked, swam, and rowed his boat on the lake. He never forgot his goal to be healthy and strong, and he never lost his enthusiasm for the plan he had made.

Of course Teddy was enthusiastic about many other things besides exercise and the outdoors. For instance, he loved to read and study, and he loved to travel. He was lucky because his family took many trips to interesting places. Teddy wanted to know everything there was to know about every country in the world. That was impossible, but he read as many books as he could about the countries his family visited.

As a matter of fact, he was so enthusiastic about so many different things that he hated to leave anything behind when it was time to go somewhere else. When his family took him on a trip, his mother kept a close eye on his packing. If she didn't, he was apt to pull his clothes out of his trunk to make room for all kinds of other interesting things.

One time while they were traveling in Europe, he pulled out most of his clothes to make room for a big collection of rocks he had gathered.

"Theodore!" his mother told him. "You need clothes to wear on this trip—not rocks to look at! Now take those rocks out of your trunk and put your clothes back in."

But as Teddy's mother took the rocks out of the trunk, Teddy slipped them into his pockets. Soon every pocket he had was bulging at the seams. His mother shook her head.

"It's fine to love nature, Theodore," she told him. "But you have to learn to leave some of it where you find it. Those rocks do *not* belong in your pockets—at least, not all of them."

THINK ABOUT IT

1. Why is it important to have enthusiasm if you want to do difficult things?
2. What are some of the things you are enthusiastic about?

TEDDY GROWS UP

By the time Teddy was eighteen, his hard work had paid off. He was strong enough to take part in any sport he liked—even boxing. And quite often he won. But his greatest fun was always hiking in the woods and riding horses. He had a good friend named Bill Sewall who was a true woodsman. Bill invited Teddy to go with him on a long camping trip into the wilderness area of Maine. This turned out to be one of the happiest summers of Teddy's life. It led to a lifelong friendship with the wilderness—and a lifelong friendship with Bill Sewall, too.

"You're a real outdoorsman, Ted," Bill told him. "If I didn't know better, I'd think you had been doing this all your life. All the men are talking about how well you fit in here. You never shirk your share of anything, no matter how tired you are. That's important when other people are depending on you."

Teddy grinned. He didn't tell Bill he had long ago learned to keep going when he felt he was too tired—even when he was doing things a lot less interesting than camping in the Maine woods!

"I'm so glad to be here that I guess I never noticed the hard work," he said. "I feel like I could never get enough of camping and exploration."

In fact, Teddy liked camping and outdoor exploration so much that he decided to become a naturalist. A naturalist is someone who studies plants and animals, especially out in nature where they live.

Teddy had always studied hard with his teachers at home, and his grades had always been high. In 1876 he was accepted as a student at Harvard University.

He decorated his apartment with birds that he had collected and mounted himself. His enthusiasm for nature led him to gather some strange roommates—snakes, insects, and other unusual animals. One time a friend who was coming to his room almost tripped over a huge tortoise slowly making its way down the hall.

"Oh, I'm glad you found him for me," Teddy said. "I guess he's looking for a drink of water."

One day his old friend Bill Sewall came to visit.

"How do you like school?" Bill asked.

"Well, in some ways I like it even better than I thought I would," Teddy answered. "But in other ways, I have to admit I'm disappointed. I thought if I studied to become a naturalist, I could spend a lot of time outdoors—like we did on our camping trip through the woods of Maine. But ideas are changing. Now everyone is more interested in studying with a microscope than studying in the fields. I'm not sure I want to spend my life in a laboratory."

"I never knew anyone smarter than you or who gets along better with all kinds of people," Bill said. "Have you ever thought of going into politics? I think you could do a lot of good in government."

The more Teddy thought about Bill's idea, the better he liked it. He liked meeting people, and he liked fighting for what he believed in. He had visited many different countries, and he had some strong ideas about what was right for America.

But first he had his studies to finish. He was also writing a book, *The Naval War of 1812*. In 1880 Teddy graduated from Harvard with honors for his high grades. That same year he married Alice Hathaway Lee, a beautiful young woman he loved very much. Two years later, in 1882, he finished his book, and it was given high praise in both England and America.

It was also in 1882 that he decided to run for election to the New York legislature. He walked all through the district knocking on doors and telling people what he believed in. He had many friends who were eager to help him, and when election day finally came, the results of Teddy's enthusiasm showed in an exciting victory. He was only 23 years old, but soon everyone was talking about this courageous young man who worked on every problem with all his heart. His energy and sense of fair play were catching, and many good laws were passed. By the time he was 25, he was recognized as an outstanding leader by men many years older than he was.

But 1884 was a very sad year for Teddy. In February the young wife he loved so dearly suddenly died, and only twelve hours later his mother died too. His term of office in the New York legislature was over, so he decided to leave the city and go back to an outdoor life until his sorrow was healed.

The prairies of North Dakota had many happy memories for Teddy. The first time he went there, several years before, he found two old buffalo hunters and asked them to take him buffalo hunting. They looked at the young Easterner who was so carefully dressed, then stepped aside to talk about their decision.

"Do you think he could stand the trip?" one asked. "He doesn't look like he's ever been far from a town."

"I don't know," the other said. "There's something about the set of his jaw—and he sure does seem enthusiastic. I say let's give him a chance."

That night they discovered their decision was a good one. When darkness fell the three men were asleep, each with his head on his saddle for a pillow. They had tied their horses to the saddle horns to keep them from wandering away.

Suddenly a pack of howling wolves came running toward the camp. The horses ran wildly in every direction, jerking the saddles out from under the sleeping men. Teddy was up and after the runaways faster than anyone. After that the hunters knew they had a brave hunting companion who would take both the good and the bad without grumbling. The three men spent many happy hours around the campfire before their hunting trip was over.

Teddy liked North Dakota so well that before returning to New York he bought a large piece of land there. Now, as he thought about where he should go, he decided he would go back to that piece of land and live the hard but peaceful life of a rancher.

One day as he was walking on a hill above the Little Missouri River, he found the interlocked antlers of two big bull elk that had fought to their death. There he built himself a log house and called his home the Elkhorn Ranch. He bought a large herd of cattle and sent for his old friend from the Maine woods, Bill Sewall. They worked long hours together, and their friendship became stronger than ever. It wasn't an easy life, but Teddy was so enthusiastic about learning to run his new ranch that he enjoyed the hardships as well as the joys.

When storms of lightning and thunder raged, the cowboys had to stay close to the cattle so they wouldn't stampede. At these times Teddy was often in his saddle for 24 hours at a time. Sometimes he had to sleep in the snow, wrapped in his blanket without even a tent over his head. In this rough life he grew stronger and more vigorous than before.

Often he would go off alone for days, hunting or fishing for his food. He always took along something to read, and in his spare moments he wrote another book of history called *The Winning of the West*.

One night in 1886 he was reading an Eastern newspaper in front of the roaring fire at Elkhorn Ranch. He was surprised to read that he had been nominated for mayor of New York.

"You know," he said, "I think maybe it's time I left the ranch and went back to see what's happening in politics."

His friend tried to hide a big grin. For quite a while he had been thinking the same thing.

THINK ABOUT IT

1. How do you think the many things Teddy was enthusiastic about when he was young helped him when he grew up?
2. Have you ever done something that took a long time and a lot of hard work? How did you feel when you were finished?

TEDDY MOVES TO THE WHITE HOUSE

Teddy Roosevelt was 28 years old when he returned to New York. He worked hard in his campaign to be elected mayor, but he was defeated. In politics as well as in ranching he had learned to take the bad with the good and keep smiling. "Well, we made a lively campaign of it anyway," he laughed. "We'll make an even livelier one next time."

He decided to take a long trip to England while he made plans for the future. It was fortunate that he did because while he was there he met an old childhood friend, Edith Kermit Carow. On December 2, 1886, they were married in London. Soon afterwards the young couple returned to the United States.

Teddy and Edith were very happy together. "I think I have the happiest home life of any man I ever knew," Teddy said to one of his good friends. His friend agreed. "I think heaven must be a little like your home," he said.

Teddy already had one young daughter, Alice, who was born to his first wife before she died. Edith was a good mother to Alice. She was also a good mother to the four sons and one daughter that were born to her and Teddy. Their names were Theodore, Kermit, Archibald, Quentin, and Ethel.

As the years passed Teddy had many opportunities to serve the people. First he was the Civil Service Commissioner, then he was president of the Police Commission of the City of New York. In 1897 he became Assistant Secretary of the Navy.

Whatever job he was given to do, he did it with all his heart. The people of America began to take notice. "That Teddy Roosevelt isn't afraid to fight for what he feels is right!" they said. "He stands up for what's fair wherever he goes!"

Teddy began to believe that soon America would have to stand up for what it felt was right. He knew Spain was getting ready to attack Cuba, a close neighbor of the United States. If it did, he was certain the United States would be drawn into the fighting too. He was right. Before long word came that the United States' battleship *Maine* had been sunk in the harbor of Havana, and the Spanish-American War had begun.

Teddy resigned his job as Assistant Secretary of the Navy. "I'm going to go to Cuba," he said. "I can't ask other men to fight in a war I'm not fighting in myself."

He had a plan to recruit volunteers from the plains and mountains he had always loved. "Those men can do any job there is to do," he told his friends in government. "They won't give up, no matter how rough things get."

Teddy was so enthusiastic about his idea that his energy and excitement spread all over the United States. Soon volunteers poured in by the thousands—cowboys and buffalo hunters, riverboat gamblers and Texas Rangers, Indians, stagecoach drivers, and college athletes. People began to call the strange regiment "The Rough Riders." Teddy was made their lieutenant colonel.

When all the new troops were lined up together, Teddy told them: "If any man wants to back out, now is the time to speak. If you stay, you have to perform whatever duty is assigned to you, whatever the danger or the difficulty. You must know how to ride, to shoot, and to live in the open. If you don't mean business, say so now. There are thousands anxious to take your place."

Not one wanted to leave. Teddy had found men with the same kind of enthusiasm for doing difficult things that he had himself. They worked with him night and day, and when their marching orders finally came, their camp was wild with celebration.

The Rough Riders became America's heroes, for they fought bravely and well. And as Teddy had said, they never gave up. Once when a corporal was wounded and taken to the hospital, he sneaked out as soon as it was dark and rejoined his comrades. When another man—a cowboy—was sent to the hospital with orders to return him to the United States, he decided he was well enough to stay in spite of his wounds. He walked six miles to find his regiment.

All the while Teddy fought side-by-side with his men. They said, "He never thinks of danger for himself, he only worries about us." The famous battle of San Juan Hill made their names known to everyone back home. When the Rough Riders returned to their own country, parades and celebrations greeted them everywhere they went.

In 1898, the year Teddy was 40 years old, he was elected Governor of New York. He was such a strong and honest governor that he was asked to be a candidate for Vice President of the United States. For a long time he refused; he liked the work he was doing in New York. But so many friends talked to him that finally he decided to campaign with William McKinley in the presidential election. Many of his Rough Riders went with him on the campaign trail, and when the election was over, McKinley had won.

But McKinley had been in office only six months when a terrible thing happened. He was shot by an assassin and died.

At forty-two years old Teddy found himself the youngest man ever to be President of the United States. "It is a very sad event that has put me in this office," he said, "but I give my pledge of honor to do all that is within my power to do."

Once again Teddy proved to be a strong and exciting leader. "Teddy Roosevelt is a joyous president," one man said. "I never saw anyone with so much enthusiasm. He has read more books, written more books, received more visitors, made more speeches, entertained more guests, taken more tours, and been interested in more sports than any other president. I don't think there is any end to his energy."

His old friend Bill Sewall came to see him, and he discovered that Teddy was the same in the White House as he was everywhere else. He romped and played with his children and, when his wife wasn't looking, they even had furious pillow fights. He taught them all to not be afraid of anything, and he taught them to love nature, too. A little girl in Kansas gave the family a badger, and other friends around the world gave them a lion, a hyena, a wild cat, a coyote, two parrots, five bears, an eagle, an owl, a zebra, and many snakes, lizards, kangaroo rats, flying squirrels, and guinea pigs.

"What are you going to do with all these animals?" Bill asked him.

Teddy smiled. "I imagine the zoo will be glad to give them a good home after the children have had a chance to get acquainted with them."

When Teddy's second term as President was finished, he decided not to run for the same office again. "Three terms as President of the United States is too much power for any man," he said. He decided to follow a dream he had had since he was in college. He went to Africa to hunt big game and to gather trophies for the Smithsonian Institution. His son Kermit went with him. Teddy sat on a seat over the cowcatcher of the train that carried them deep into the African wilderness. He was as excited as a young boy over all the strange birds and animals they were seeing. He spent almost a year in Africa, and he liked the country so well that his sons nicknamed him "The Lion."

On the way home to America he traveled through Europe. Everywhere he went, kings and other leaders who had admired him as President of the United States showed him great honor.

Teddy took other trips seeking adventure. In 1913 he went on a great scientific expedition to the jungles of Brazil, where a river was named Rio Teodoro in his honor. But his health was gradually failing, and he was never well again after that hard journey. On January 6, 1919, he worked on his papers awhile, then he went to bed for the last time. The next morning his son sent word to the other children: "The Lion is dead."

Messages came from people all over the world who shared his family's sorrow. "He delighted all people everywhere with his bold and dramatic personality," one man wrote. "He was a most unusual president," said another. "He didn't need some terrible crisis to make him seem important—whatever he was doing, you knew he was a great man." Still another wrote, "I think there has never been another person with such courage and enthusiasm. Everything Teddy Roosevelt did, he did with all his heart."